MY FIRST
ITALIAN
PHRASES

Can we go out to eat?
Possiamo andare fuori a cena?
(pohs-see-AH-moh ahn-DAH-ray FOOHO-ree ah CHAYN-nah)

I don't like strawberry ice cream.
Non mi piace il gelato alla fragola.
(nohn mee pee-AH-chay eel ay-LAH-toh AHL-lah FRAH-go-lah)

BY
JILL KALZ

ILLUSTRATED BY
DANIELE FABBRI

TRANSLATED BY
TRANSLATIONS.COM

PICTURE WINDOW BOOKS
a capstone imprint

TABLE OF
CONTENTS

HOW TO USE THIS DICTIONARY

This book is full of useful phrases in both English and Italian. The English phrase appears first, followed by the Italian phrase. Look below each Italian phrase for help to sound it out. Try reading the phrases aloud.

Topic heading in English

English: THE BASICS

Hello.
Ciao.
(CHOW)

Good morning.
Buongiorno.
(bwon-JOR-noh)

Good night.
Buona notte.
(BWO-nah NOHT-tay)

Good afternoon.
Buon pomeriggio.
(bwon poh-may-REE-joh)

Excuse me.
Scusa.
(SKOO-zah)

Good-bye.
Arrivederci.
(ah-ree-vay-DAYR-chee)

Please.
Per favore.
(payr fah-VOH-ray)

Italian: I FONDAMENTALI (ee fon-dah-mayn-TAH)

Thank you.
Grazie.
(GRAH-zeeoy)

You are welcome.
Prego.
(PRAY-goh)

What is your name?
Come ti chiami?
(KOH-may tee kee-AH-mee)

My name is ___.
Mi chiamo ___.
(mee kee-AH-moh ___)

MORE TO LEARN

Yes — **Sì** (see)
No — **No** (noh)

Topic heading in Italian

Additional phrases to learn

Phrase in English
Phrase in Italian
(pronunciation)

NOTES ABOUT THE ITALIAN LANGUAGE

In the Italian language, nouns are masculine or feminine. The Italian words for "a," "an," "the," and "some" tell a noun's gender and number. Here is a quick reference guide:

English word	Masculine	Plural	Feminine	Plural
a/an	un/uno		una/un'	
the	il/lo	i/gli	la	le
some		alcuni		alcune

Adjectives can be placed before or after a noun. Adjectives ending in "o" have four forms, according to gender and number. For example, the word "happy" is written as "allegro" if the speaker is male and "allegra" if the speaker is female.

In this phrase book, the phrases match the gender of the characters shown on each page.

LETTERS OF THE ALPHABET
AND THEIR PRONUNCIATIONS

A a • ah   B b • bee   C c • chee

D d • dee   E e • ay   F f • EF-fay

G g • jee   H h • AHK-kah   I i • ee

L l • EL-lay   M m • EM-may   N n • EN-nay

O o • oh   P p • pee   Q q • ku

R r • AYR-ray   S s • ES-say   T t • tee

U u • oo   V v • voo   Z z • DZAY-tah

IT SOUNDS LIKE

There are 21 letters in the Italian alphabet. The Italian letters are the same letters found in the English alphabet. The letters "j," "k," "w," "x," and "y" are not used. They do appear in foreign words, such as "jeans." Some of the letters sound similar to English letters. But some letters and letter combinations sound much different, or are silent. Use this guide to learn how to say these sounds. Look at the pronunciations to help you sound out the words.

	SOUND	PRONUNCIATION	EXAMPLES
CONSONANTS	c	if followed by a, o, or u, like c in cat; if followed by i or e, like ch in church	candela kan-DAY-lah circo CHEER-coh
	g	if followed by a, o, or u, like g in gas; if followed by e or i, like g in giraffe	gondola GOHN-doh-lah ginnasta jeen-NAH-stah
	gl	like lli in million	famiglia fah-MEE-lyah
	gn	like ni in onion	Bologna boh-LOH-nyah
	sc	if followed by a, o, or u, like sk in skunk; if followed by e or i, like sh in she	scatola SKAH-toh-lah sci SHEE
	qu	like c in cooler	quando KWAHN-doh
	z	like ts in spits	zebra TSAY-brah
	h	always silent	hotel oh-TAYL
	double letters	make the sound of the double letter longer	letto LAYT-toh
VOWELS	a	like a in father	mamma MAHM-mah
	e	like ay in may	felice fay-LEE-chay
	i	like ee in keen	triste TREES-tay
	o	like o in boy	nero NAY-roh
	u	like u in rude	blu BLOO
	è	like e in set	perchè payr-KEH
	à, è, ò, ì, ù	Always found at the end of a word. Stress the accent on the last syllable.	lunedì loo-nay-DEE sarò sah-ROH
VOWEL COMBINATIONS	ia	like ya in yard	ciglia CHEE-lya
	io	like yo in yoyo	coniglio coh-NEE-lyo
	ie	like ye in yen	iena YE-nah
	ai	like ey in eyes	bonsai bohn-SYE
	ei	like ey in grey	nei NAY-ee

English: THE BASICS

Italian: I FONDAMENTALI (ee fon-dah-mayn-TAH-lee)

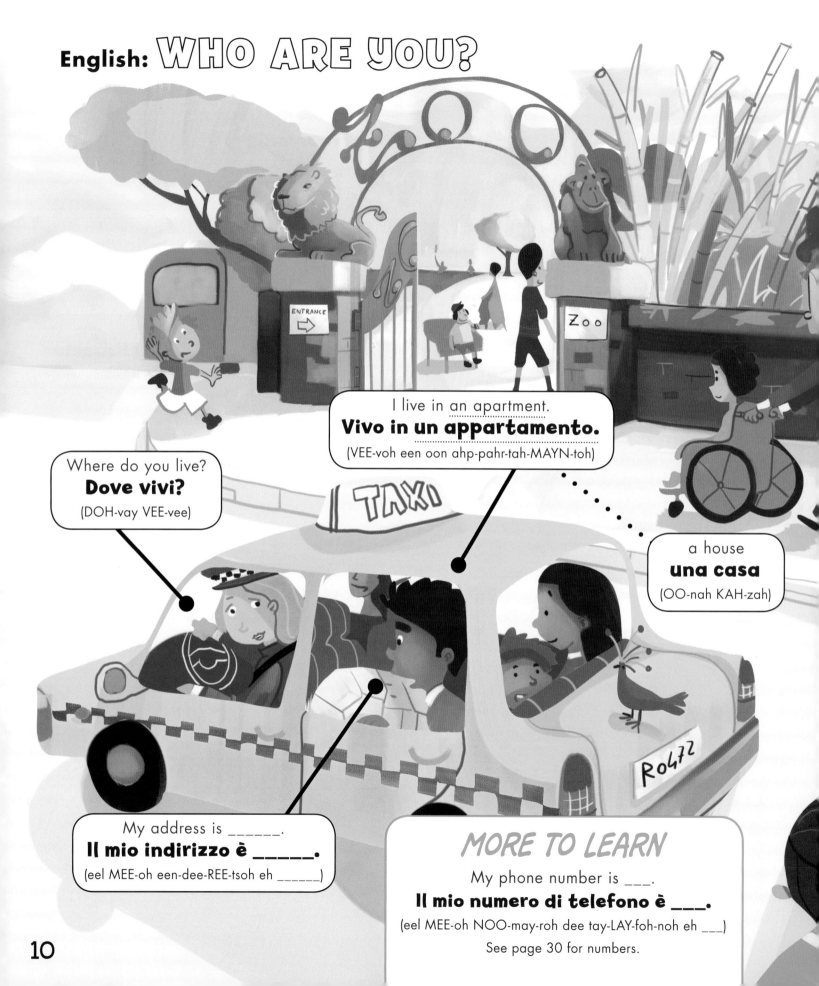

I live in an apartment.
Vivo in un appartamento.
(VEE-voh een oon ahp-pahr-tah-MAYN-toh)

Where do you live?
Dove vivi?
(DOH-vay VEE-vee)

a house
una casa
(OO-nah KAH-zah)

My address is _____.
Il mio indirizzo è _____.
(eel MEE-oh een-dee-REE-tsoh eh _____)

MORE TO LEARN
My phone number is ___.
Il mio numero di telefono è ___.
(eel MEE-oh NOO-may-roh dee tay-LAY-foh-noh eh ___)
See page 30 for numbers.

English: **MEALS**

Are you hungry?
Hai fame?
(AH-ee FAH-may)

I am hungry.
Ho fame.
(oh FAH-may)

thirsty
sete
(SAY-tay)

What is for supper?
Cosa c'è per cena?
(KO-za cheh per CHEH-nah)

lunch
pranzo
(PRAHN-zoh)

breakfast
colazione
(ko-lah-zee-OH-nay)

MORE TO LEARN

I am not hungry.
Non ho fame.
(nohn oh FAH-may)

Italian: PASTI (PAHS-tee)

Can we go out to eat?
Possiamo andare fuori a cena?
(pohs-see-AH-moh ahn-DAH-ray FOOHO-ree ah CHAYN-nah)

I like Chinese food.
Mi piace il cibo cinese.
(mee pee-AH-chay eel CHI-boh chee-NAY-zay)

I don't like strawberry ice cream.
Non mi piace il gelato alla fragola.
(nohn mee pee-AH-chay eel jay-LAH-toh AHL-lah FRAH-go-lah)

Italian: FAMIGLIA (fah-MEE-lyah)

Do you speak English?
Parli inglese?
(PAHR-lee een-GLEH-say)

Spanish
spagnolo
(spa-NYOH-loh)

German
tedesco
(tay-DEH-skoh)

French
francese
(frahn-CHAY-zay)

Chinese
cinese
(chee-NAY-zay)

DUTY FREE

7 8 9 10 11 12

A little.
Un po'.
(oon poh)

MORE TO LEARN

father
padre
(PAH-dray)

sister
sorella
(soh-REHL-lah)

brother
fratello
(frah-TEHL-loh)

15

It is time to get up.
È ora di alzarsi.
(EH OH-rah dee ahl-ZAR-see)

What time is it?
Che ore sono?
(keh OH-ray SOH-noh)

It is time to go to bed.
È ora di andare a letto.
(EH OH-rah dee ahn-DAH-ray ah LEHT-toh)

When are we leaving?
Quando andiamo?
(KWAHN-doh ahn-dee-AH-moh)

Italian: DATA E ORA (DAH-tah ay OH-rah)

Today is Saturday.
Oggi è sabato.
(OHJ-jee eh SAH-bah-toh)

Tomorrow is Sunday.
Domani è domenica.
(doh-MAH-nee eh doh-MAY-nee-kah)

Yesterday was Friday.
Ieri era venerdì.
(ee-AY-ree AY-rah vay-nayr-DEE)

MORE TO LEARN

Sunday
domenica
(doh-MAY-nee-kah)

Monday
lunedì
(loo-nay-DEE)

Tuesday
martedì
(mahr-tay-DEE)

Wednesday
mercoledì
(mehr-koh-lay-DEE)

Thursday
giovedì
(jo-vay-DEE)

Friday
venerdì
(vay-nayr-DEE)

Saturday
sabato
(SAH-bah-toh)

Happy birthday!
Buon compleanno!
(bwon kohm-play-AHN-noh)

When is your birthday?
Quando è il tuo compleanno?
(KWAHN-doh eh eel TOO-oh kohm-play-AHN-noh)

My birthday is in May.
Il mio compleanno è in maggio.
(eel MEE-oh kohm-play-AHN-noh eh een MAHJ-joh)

Italian: MESI E STAGIONI (MAY-see EH stah-JOH-nee)

I love summer!
Mi piace l'estate!
(mee pee-AH-chay lay-STAH-tay)

fall
autunno
(a-hoo-TOON-noh)

winter
inverno
(een-VEHR-noh)

spring
primavera
(pree-mah-VAY-rah)

MORE TO LEARN

January
gennaio
(jayn-NAH-yoh)

February
febbraio
(fayb-BRAH-yoh)

March
marzo
(MAHR-zoh)

April
aprile
(ah-PREE-lay)

May
maggio
(MAHJ-joh)

June
giugno
(JU-nyoh)

July
luglio
(LU-yoh)

August
agosto
(ah-GOH-stoh)

September
settembre
(sayt-TAYM-bray)

October
ottobre
(oht-TOH-bray)

November
novembre
(noh-VAYM-bray)

December
dicembre
(dee-CHAYM-bray)

It is cold.
Fa freddo.
(fah FRED-doh)

hot
caldo
(KAHL-doh)

It is sunny.
È soleggiato.
(eh soh-layj-JEEAH-toh)

Wear a coat.
Metti un cappotto.
(MAYT-tee oon kahp-POHT-toh)

boots
gli stivali
(yee stee-VAH-lee)

hat
il cappello
(eel kahp-PEHL-loh)

gloves
i guanti
(ee goo-AHN-tee)

21

Italian: SCUOLA (sku-OH-lah)

Where is the bathroom?
Dov'è il bagno?
(doh-VEH eel BAH-nyoh)

lunchroom
la sala mensa
(lah SAH-lah MAYN-sah)

bus stop
la fermata del bus
(lah fayr-MAH-tah dayl boos)

Go right.
Vai a destra.
(VAH-ee ah DAYS-trah)

straight ahead
dritto
(DREET-toh)

left
a sinistra
(ah see-NEE-strah)

Are you ready for the test?
Sei pronto per la verifica?
(SAY-ee PROHN-toh payr lah vay-REE-fee-kah)

I forgot.
Mi sono dimenticato.
(mee SOH-noh dee-mayn-tee-KAH-toh)

Do you play sports?
Pratichi qualche sport?
(PRAH-tee-kee KWAHL-kay sport)

I play <u>baseball</u>.
Gioco a baseball.
(JEEOH-koh ah BAYS-bohl)

basketball
basket
(BAS-kayt)

football
football americano
(FOOT-bol ah-mayr-ee-KAH-noh)

soccer
calcio
(CAL-cheeoh)

I won.
Ho vinto.
(oh VEEN-toh)

I lost.
Ho perso.
(oh PEHR-soh)

Congratulations!
Bravo!
(BRAH-voh)

Italian: CON GLI AMICI (kon yee ah-MEE-chee)

Numbers • **NUMERI** (NOO-may-ree)

1 one • **uno** (OO-noh)

2 two • **due** (DOO-ay)

3 three • **tre** (TRAY)

4 four • **quattro** (KOOAT-troh)

5 five • **cinque** (CHIN-kuay)

6 six • **sei** (SAY-ee)

7 seven • **sette** (SEHT-teh)

8 eight • **otto** (OHT-toh)

9 nine • **nove** (NOH-vay)

10 ten • **dieci** (DEEAY-chee)

11 eleven • **undici** (OON-dee-chee)

12 twelve • **dodici** (DOH-dee-chee)

13 thirteen • **tredici** (TRAY-dee-chee)

14 fourteen • **quattordici** (KWAH-tor-dee-chee)

15 fifteen • **quindici** (QUEEN-dee-chee)

16 sixteen • **sedici** (SAY-dee-chee)

17 seventeen • **diciassette** (dee-chah-SAYT–tay)

18 eighteen • **diciotto** (dee-CHOHT-toh)

19 nineteen • **diciannove** (dee-chah-NOH-vay)

20 twenty • **venti** (VAYN-tee)

30 thirty • **trenta** (TRAYN-tah)

40 forty • **quaranta** (kooa-RAHN-tah)

50 fifty • **cinquanta** (chin-KOOAHN-tah)

60 sixty • **sessanta** (sehs-SAHN-tah)

70 seventy • **settanta** (seht-TAHN-tah)

80 eighty • **ottanta** (oht-TAHN-tah)

90 ninety • **novanta** (noh-VAHN-tah)

100 one hundred • **cento** (CHAYN-toh)

Colors • COLORI (koh-LOH-ree)

 red • **rosso**
(ROHS-soh)

 purple • **viola**
(vee-OH-lah)

 orange • **arancione**
(ah-ran-CHYOHN-nay)

 pink • **rosa**
(ROH-zah)

yellow • **giallo**
(JIAL-loh)

 brown • **marrone**
(mahr-ROH-nay)

 green • **verde**
(VAYR-day)

 black • **nero**
(NAY-roh)

 blue • **blu**
(BLOO)

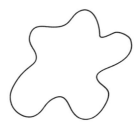 white • **bianco**
(bee-AHN-koh)

READ MORE

Kudela, Katy R. *My First Book of Italian Words.* Bilingual Picture Dictionaries. Mankato, Minn.: Capstone Press, 2010.

Mahoney, Judy. *Teach Me—Everyday Italian.* Teach Me—. Minnetonka, Minn.: Teach Me Tapes, 2008.

Medina, Sarah. *Italian.* Languages of the World. Chicago: Heinemann Library, 2012.

INTERNET SITES

FactHound offers a safe, fun way to find Internet sites related to this book. All of the sites on FactHound have been researched by our staff.

Here's all you do:

Visit *www.facthound.com*

Type in this code: 9781404875166

 **Super-cool stuff!** Check out projects, games and lots more at **www.capstonekids.com**

LOOK FOR ALL THE BOOKS IN THE SPEAK ANOTHER LANGUAGE SERIES:

MY FIRST ARABIC PHRASES

MY FIRST FRENCH PHRASES

MY FIRST GERMAN PHRASES

MY FIRST ITALIAN PHRASES

MY FIRST JAPANESE PHRASES

MY FIRST MANDARIN CHINESE PHRASES

MY FIRST RUSSIAN PHRASES

MY FIRST SPANISH PHRASES

Thanks to our adviser for his expertise, research, and advice:
Eric Dregni, Dean of Lago del Bosco,
The Italian Concordia Language Village

Editor: Shelly Lyons
Set Designer: Alison Thiele
Production Designer: Eric Manske
Art Director: Nathan Gassman
Production Specialist: Laura Manthe
The illustrations in this book were created digitally.

Picture Window Books
1710 Roe Crest Drive
North Mankato, Minnesota 56003
877-845-8392
www.capstonepub.com

Library of Congress Cataloging-in-Publication Data
Kalz, Jill.
My first Italian phrases / by Jill Kalz ; illustrations by Daniele Fabbri.
    pages. cm.— (Capstone picture window books)
ISBN 978-1-4048-7516-6 (library binding)
ISBN 978-1-4048-7736-8 (paperback)
ISBN 978-1-4048-7996-6 (ebook PDF)
1. Italian language—Textbooks. I. Title. II. Series: Capstone picture window books.
 PC1112.5.K359 2013
 458.3'421—dc23   2012002516

Summary: Simple text paired with themed illustrations invite the reader to learn to speak Italian.—Provided by publisher.

Printed in the United States of America in North Mankato, Minnesota.
042012   006682CGF12